A Far Side collection

THE CHICKENS ARE RESTLESS

Other Books in The Far Side Series

The Far Side
Beyond The Far Side
In Search of The Far Side
Bride of The Far Side
Valley of The Far Side
It Came From The Far Side
Hound of The Far Side
The Far Side Observer
Night of the Crash-Test Dummies
Wildlife Preserves
Wiener Dog Art
Unnatural Selections
Cows of Our Planet

Anthologies

The Far Side Gallery
The Far Side Gallery 2
The Far Side Gallery 3
The Far Side Gallery 4

Retrospective

The PreHistory of The Far Side: A 10th Anniversary Exhibit

A Far Side collection by Gary Larson

THE CHICKENS ARE RESTLESS

Andrews and McMeel
A Universal Press Syndicate Company
Kansas City

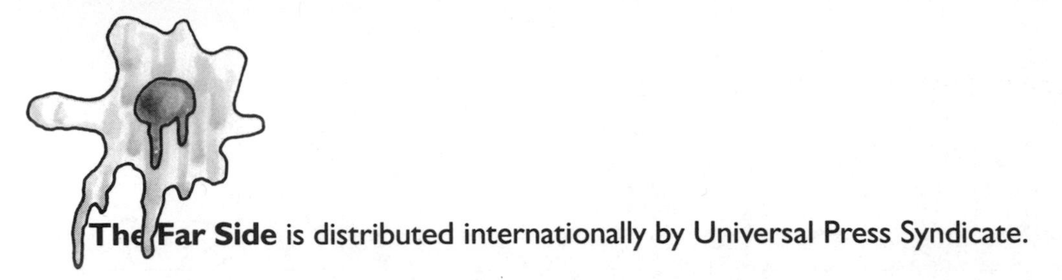

The Far Side is distributed internationally by Universal Press Syndicate.

 For information write Andrews and McMeel, a Universal Press Syndicate Company, 4900 Main Street, Kansas City, Missouri 64112.

ISBN: 0-8362-1717-9
Library of Congress Catalog Card Number: 93-71010

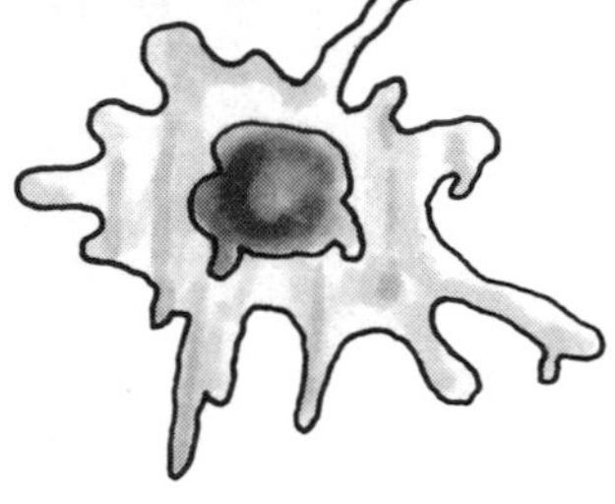

Printed on recycled paper.

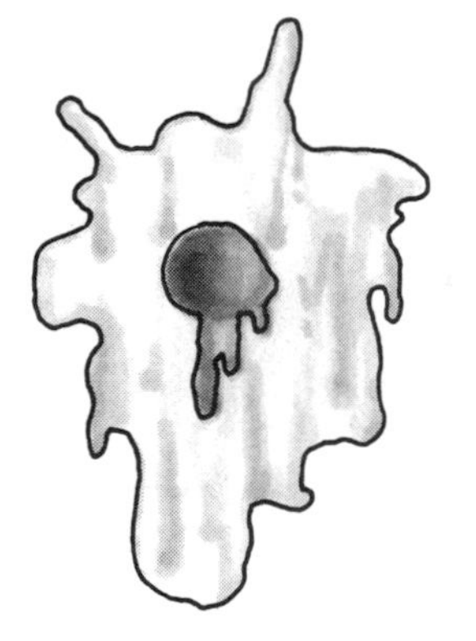

"Confession time, Mona: I've led you astray."

"Mmmmmm ... interesting ... interesting. ... I'd say we taste a little like chicken."

And for the rest of his life, Ernie told his friends that he had talked with God.

To the horror of the lifeboat's other members, Madonna loses her balance and falls on her face.

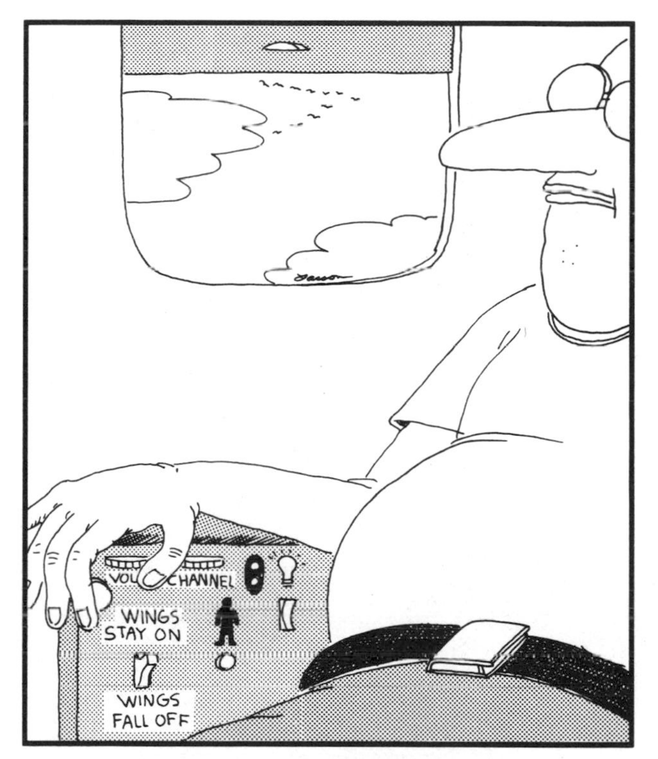

Fumbling for his recline button, Ted unwittingly instigates a disaster.

"God, Collings, I hate to start a Monday with a case like this."

At Slow Cheetahs Anonymous

"OK, boys — that'll be enough.
We don't allow any gunplay in this town."

“OK, time for lunch. … And Dwayne here will be dismissing you by row number, since he’s alpha wolf today.”

The living hell of Maurice, Jacques Cousteau’s cat

Red Cloud's ultimate nightmare

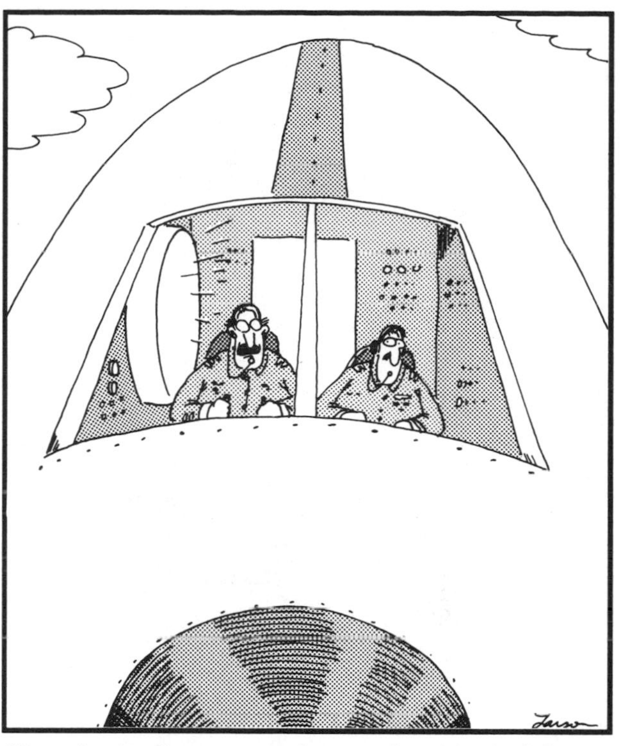

"I'm afraid we're going to have to head back, folks. ... We've got a warning light on up here, and darn if it isn't the big one."

Larson
Dumb bunny.
Smart ass.
ANIMAL FARM

Larson
BLIND
And tails cut off with a carving Knife

"Amazing! The mummified remains of a prehistoric cave-painter — still clutching his brush! ... Seems he made an enemy, though."

The Viking longcar was once the scourge of European roadways.

A Louvre guard is suddenly unsettled by the arrival of Linda Blair.

"Remember, Calloway, this is their biggest and best warrior — so stay alert! When you knock him down, he's going to come right back at you!"

"Abdul, my old friend! Come in! Come in! Have you traveled far?!"

Origin of the expression, "Putting on the dog"

Hummingbirds, of course, have to watch nature films
with the action greatly speeded up.

"As you can see, most of these things are jackrabbits, but keep your eyes peeled for armadillo as well. ... We're about five miles now from the dead steer."

Although never achieving the fame of his African counterpart, Larry of the Lemurs was a common sight to natives of Madagascar.

Bored dogs are often subject to the phenomenon of cat mirages.

Pickpockets of the Rue Morgue

Tarantula coffeehouses

"OK, Mr. Hook. Seems you're trying to decide between a career in pirating or massage therapy. Well, maybe we can help you narrow it down."

"We can't go on like this, Ramone. ... One day, George is bound to take his blinders off."

With the surgical team passed out, and with help from the observation deck, hospital custodian Leonard Knudson suddenly became responsible for bringing Mr. Gruenfeld "home."

"Well, there goes Binky with the boss again. ... What a red-noser!"

She was known as Madame D'Gizarde, and, in the early '40s, she used deceit, drugs, and her beguiling charms to become the bane of chicken farmers everywhere.

"*His* story? Well, I dunno. ... I always assumed he was just a bad dog."

Scene from *Dr. Jekyll and Mr. Ed*

Again the doorbell chimed. With his wife out of town, and not expecting any visitors, Mohammed began to grow uneasy.

Popeye on the dating scene

Wellington held out some beads and other trinkets, but the islanders had sent their fiercest lawyers — some of whom were chanting, "Sue him! Sue him!"

Trouble brewing

The writers for "Bewitched" sit down to their weekly brainstorming session.

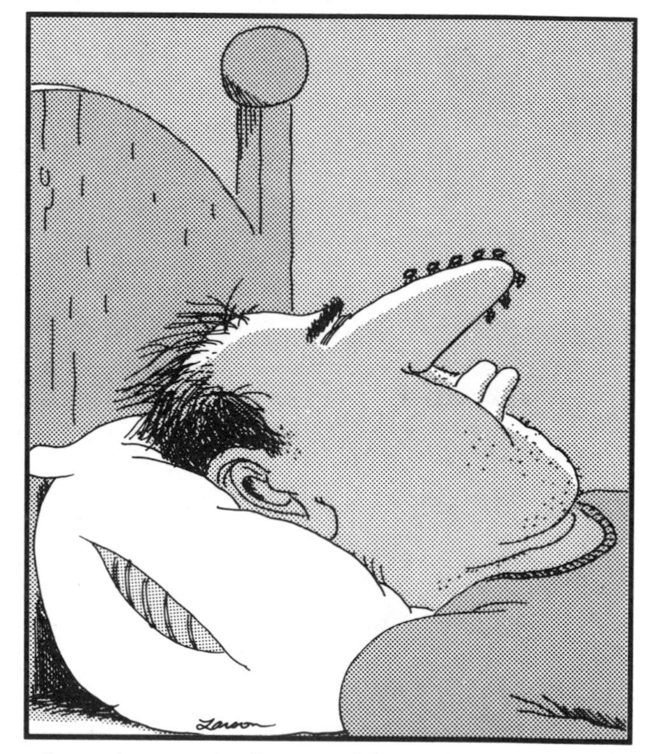

Every August, the fleas would test their endurance in the grueling Tour de Frank.

"AAAAAAAAAA! It's Sid! Someone snuffed him!"

Where the respective worlds of boating and herpetology converge.

As witnesses later recalled, two small dogs just waltzed into the place, grabbed the cat, and waltzed out.

Testifying before a Senate subcommittee, the Hardy boys crack the Iran-contra scandal.

"Go ahead and jump, Sid! Hell — I *know* you're thinkin' it!"

"Oh, it's just Hank's little cross to bear — he's allergic to down and that's that."

As his eyes grew accustomed to the dark, Death suddenly noticed his girlfriend sitting with Dr. Jack Kevorkian.

Every year, hundreds of tourists travel great distances to get a glimpse of the few remaining mountain chihuahuas.

The curse of songwriter's block

"Now now now. ... You won't be a lonely road forever, you know."

Long before his show-business career, he was known as Mr. Liberace, the wood-shop teacher.

The ever-popular Donner Party snow dome

"Fifty bucks?" I said. "Hey! Do I look like I got a hole in my head?" ...But seriously, folks...
Larson

Larson
Bottom of the pecking order, eh?... Oh, I don't think so... Ha ha ha ha ha ha!

"Well, I'll be. ... I must've been holding the dang work order like *this*!"

"OK, ma'am you said you warned your husband to put the newspaper down or you'd blow him away. ... Did he respond?"

It was always a bizarre spectacle, but no one ever, *ever*, ridiculed the Teapot Kid.

And then the bovine watchers were given a *real* treat. On a small knoll, in full splendor, there suddenly appeared a Guatemalan cow of paradise.

"Boy, everyone's really out wandering the streets tonight. ... I tell you, Charles, we're getting to be real home zombies."

Monday night in the woods

Moses parting his hair

"We're screwed, Marge. Big Al was our star attraction, the king of the show. ... And now he's gone."

Unbeknownst to most students of psychology, Pavlov's first experiment was to ring a bell and cause his dog to attack Freud's cat.

"Don't touch it, honey ... it's just a face in the crowd."

The Angel of Migraines

It was a tough frontier town; but later, after the arrival of the Earp brothers, things calmed down, and the town's name was shortened to simply Dodge City.

"Hey, Lola. Did you see this thing in the paper?"

FREEZER
GIZZARDS
RED HEN
POULTRY CO.
Larson

Question: If a tree falls in the forest and no one's around, and it hits a mime, does anyone care?

"Quit school? *Quit school*? You wanna end up like your father? A career lab rat?"

A tragedy occurs off the coast of a land called Honah-Lee.

"Edgar! Leave him be! ... Always best to let sleeping dogs lie."

Ichabod Crane vs. the Headless Horseman
in The People's Court

"Well, kid, ya beat me — and now every punk packin' a paddle and tryin' to make a name for himself will come lookin' for *you*! ... Welcome to hell, kid!"

Later, Edna was forced to sell her brussels sprout house.

Years later, Harold Zimmerman, the original "Hookhand" of the campfire ghost stories, tells his grandchildren the Tale of the Two Evil Teen-agers.

Suddenly, the cops stepped into the clearing, and the Spamshiners knew they were busted.

The woods were dark and foreboding,
and Alice sensed that sinister eyes were watching
her every step. Worst of all, she knew that
Nature abhorred a vacuum.

"Dogs that drink from the toilet bowl — after this."

Early plumbers

Chicken sexual fantasies

"Sheriff! Ben Wiggins is ridin' into town, and he's wearin' that same little chiffon number that he wore when he shot Jake Sutton!"

Scene from *Insurance Salesman of the Opera*

"Little Bear! A watched head never gets eaten by ants."

Historical note: For many years, until they became truly nasty, Vikings would plunder, loot, and then egg the houses of coastal villagers.

Hot off the press, the very first edition of the *Desert Island Times* caused the newspaper to quickly fold.

"Oo! *I'd* get up on that big fuzzy one!"

"So Mr. Pig — you built that fire *after* you heard my client coming down your chimney! ... Did you know my client is an endangered species, Mr. Pig, while you yourself are nothing more than a walking side of ham?"

The magnificent Lippizaner cows

Tapeworms on vacation

"Look, if it was electric, could I do this?"

"Oh, the box of dead flies? Ramone gave them to me Saturday night during his courtship display. ... Of course they were already sucked dry."

"It's time we face reality, my friend. ... We're not exactly rocket scientists."

Octopus obedience school

Calf delinquents

Cossaccountants

Jurassic calendars

"And then wham! This thing just came right out of left field."

Be a virus, see the world.

On this particular day, Rory the raccoon was hunting frogs at his favorite stream, and the pleasant background music told him that Mr. Mountain Lion was nowhere around.

Tensions mount on the Lewis and Clark expedition.

Only Claire, with her oversized brain, wore an expression of concern.

"Excuse me, sir, but could your entire family please step out of the car? ... Your faces are not in order."

"Norm? This is Mitch. ... You were right —
I found my drill."

In her past, and unbeknownst to most people, Leona Helmsley was an avid bungee jumper.

Near misses of the Old West

That night, Captain MacIntyre was killed by a following sea.

"The problem, as I see it, is that you both are extremely adept at pushing each other's buttons."

"Hey, boy! How ya doin'? ... Look at him, Dan. Poor guy's been floating out here for days but he's still just as fat and happy as ever."

Through mostly grunts and exaggerated gestures, two fishermen/gatherers attempt to communicate.

More facts of nature: All forest animals, to this very day, remember exactly where they were and what they were doing when they heard that Bambi's mother had been shot.

"One more time: You were at the park, enjoying the afternoon, when you distinctly heard the defendant turn to his dog and say: 'Look, boy! A stickman!' "

Zoombies: the driving dead

"Hey, who's that? ... Oh — Mitch, the janitor. Well, our first test run has just gotten a little more interesting."

Drive-by erasings

"In this dramatic turn of events, testimony against Mr. Pumpkineater is about to be given by his sister, Jeannie Jeannie Eatszucchini."

"He kids me ... he kids me not. ... He kids me ... he kids me not. ..."

"Professor LaVonne had many enemies in the entomological world, detective, but if you examine that data label, you'll find exactly when and where he was — shall we say — 'collected.'"

Failed marketing ploys

What the stranger didn't know, of course, was that Sam always kept a dobie in his boot.

Back in his college days, Igor was considered to be the HBOC.

"Well, lemme think. ... You've stumped me, son. Most folks only wanna know how to go the other way."

"Hey! You're not lookin' to buy anything, are you? I think you best just keep movin', buddy."

"Oh, my God! Dung beetles! ... And in their filthy dungarees, of course!"

"Of course, one of the more popular myths is that our 16th president was born in a little log cabin."

"OK, OK! Calm down, everyone! ... This monster — would you say he was bigger or smaller than your building? ... You can talk it over."

Henry VIII on the dating scene

He had seen Tanzania, and most of Mozambique was already behind him. There was no mistake. Chippy had done what most chimps only dream about: He had caught the Perfect Vine.

"I love the desert."

"You *must* be new here! ... That's Miss Crutchfield, and she's there to make sure *nobody* runs with scissors."

Careening through the neighborhood with reckless abandon, none of them suspected that Tuffy was still tied up.

"Tell me, Margaret. ... Am I a butthead?"

"Thanks for being my friend, Wayne."

Larson

At the I've Fallen and I Can't Get Up Building

Common butt stickers of the Old West

Abducted by an alien circus company, Professor Doyle is forced to write calculus equations in center ring.

Boxer nightmares

"This is it, Maurice! I've warned you to keep your hens off me!"

It was no place for yellow squash.

"Hey! You! ... Yeah, you! I ain't gonna tell you again
to quit spittin' on me!"

Early corsages

He was king of the sheep.

"Whoa whoa whoa, young man! You *walk* the plank like everyone else!"

A big day for Jimmy

Only Bernard, in the front row, had the nerve to laugh at Death.

"Be patient, Leona, be patient. ... Zebras won't take a drink until they know it's absolutely safe."

Long before his rise to fame, artist Gus Nickerson experimented with many variations on a single theme — until that fateful day when a friend said, "Gus ... have you tried *dogs* playing poker?"

"And so," the interviewer asked, "do you ever have trouble coming up with ideas?" "Well, sometimes," the cartoonist replied.